I0500269

IDEAS INTO PROFIT

8 ESSENTIAL STEPS TO HELP MAKE

YOUR BUSINESS IDEAS A REALITY.

by

Esther Wairumbi

This edition first published in United Kingdom 2017
Copyright © 2017 by Esther Wairumbi

IDEAS INTO PROFIT

8 Essential steps to help make your business ideas a reality.

ISBN : 978-1-548-82736-6

Contact Information
Email: estherwa@hotmail.com
Published in Great Britain

Published by M4LL- A part of Empowering Communities (UK) LTD

IDEAS INTO PROFIT

8 ESSENTIAL STEPS TO HELP MAKE

YOUR BUSINESS IDEAS A REALITY.

by

Esther Wairumbi

"

If you have ideas, you have the main asset you need, and there isn't any limit to what you can do with your business and your life. Ideas are any man's greatest asset.

"

Harvey S. Firestone

CONTENTS

ACKNOWLEDGMENTS

First and foremost I want to thank Almighty God for always being there and for the great people around me who have been part of this journey.

I also take this opportunity to thank my parents, my late father, John Wairumbi, and my mother, Beth Wairumbi. At an early age, they taught me how to believe in myself. I grew up watching them run their own businesses successfully, as they taught me the valuable lessons of what this entailed - hard work, focus and determination! Their extraordinary efforts and dedication to run a family business taught me the valuable business principles and dedication that I treasure to this day.

I also want to acknowledge the special people who helped me in various ways to put this book together. I could not have written it without the inspiration and encouragement of my mother Beth Wairumbi, my partner, Martin Joseph, who proof read the first draft, and my nephew Michael Gachuru, who helped in various ways in shaping this book.

I would also like to thank my University Professor of Music and founder of Apex Music company USA Boyd Gibson for the help, support and offering to read the raw draft. A big thank you.

I am indebted to all of you for being there when I needed you.

This book is also dedicated to those who are struggling to move on to the next level with their business idea; to those who feel that their dreams and aspirations are not yet bearing fruit, and feel they may need some guidance and motivation to push them a bit further.

INTRODUCTION

This easy to read book is aimed at giving entrepreneurs, start-ups, and those thinking of starting up soon, the advice, knowledge and motivation to turn their dreams and ideas into reality. This book is for you, the visionary, the entrepreneur, the big dreamer, the inventor - to monetize your dreams and ideas by starting and developing a business.

Having had an opportunity and privilege to work as a business manager in one of the world's leading banks in London, United Kingdom, for close to 10 years - where I was awarded a high achiever gold award for excellence - I have acquired a wealth of knowledge and expertise in helping entrepreneurs start and grow their businesses.

In this book I wish to share the knowledge I have gained over the years to help you get started with your ideas, and achieve your desired business goals. Many people lack confidence in turning their ideas into a viable business, and that is where I wish to help you achieve the clear vision and confidence needed to put your ideas into action.

This book will equip you with the essential and necessary knowledge needed to transform your ideas into a working business model – the business that you dream of, the one that you deserve, and the one that you can be proud to be your own boss of. Of course all of this requires your hard work, commitment, and discipline. So let's get to it!

CHAPTER
ONE

BUSINESS IDEAS

What is a business idea?

An idea is defined as a thought generated with intent.

A business idea is usually the first step in the process of building a business for financial gain through offering a product or service that can be exchanged for money.

Business idea is where all entrepreneurs start from in their journey to successful businesses. It all starts with having an idea, thinking through it and doing some research to see if the idea is viable.

There are several reasons why a business idea can come about and in the next page we are going to have a look at some examples. As you read through them try to think of opportunities around you that you can turn into viable business opportunities.

Here are some examples.

- You have identified something that is missing in the market place that people need, you spot the opportunity and runs with it.

- It could be something that exists and is not solving the existing problem adequately or is lacking in innovation.

- The solution available might also be unaffordable to a large number of people, this then gives you an idea, to provide an alternative cheaper solution to the existing problem.

- An existing problem that needs solving and one that no one has addressed yet, you then come up with an innovative idea that can solve the problem.

- It could be something that frustrates you because everyone is offering the same product or service, and you have an innovative unique solution that adds extra value and people will be willing to buy from you for your product or service unique features that stands out from the rest.

You have a business idea that you are passionate about? Great!

Apart from the financial reasons for starting a business (to make a profit) there are many reasons why people start their own businesses, just as there are many different businesses.

Here are some of the reasons business owners gave when asked why they started their own businesses.

- Desire to be own boss.

- Solve an existing problem.

- Create opportunities for themselves and others.

- Desire to work hard for something they are passionate about.

- A business legacy they can pass on to their children.

- To earn extra income while they are still in employment (create multiple streams of income).

The last category on the list above is interesting, as my research indicates that many people initially venture into business as a side hustle, to earn extra income, whilst they are still employed. This enables them to build and grow their business gradually over time, whilst still having job security.

While some people venture into business as a hobby, others turn their hobby into a money making business. Others venture into business because they have a solution to an existing problem, that no one is solving. They come up with creative ideas to meet this need.

Coming up with great business ideas is sometimes the easy part – actually putting those ideas into action can sometimes prove to be the scariest and most difficult part for most people.

Many people have viable business ideas, but very few make it their business to put their ideas into action and take it to the next level.

But take heart - turning your dreams, aspirations, and ideas into reality need not be as scary as it may feel. Once you have a viable business idea, and the drive, determination, and passion to succeed, you can achieve your desired outcome using some of the strategies covered in this book.

When I worked as a business manager in one of the leading banks in London, I came across enterprising people with great business ideas, but many of those ideas remained dormant because no action was taken beyond gathering information and brainstorming the ideas. There were various reasons for this, but often, it was due to people not following through with their dreams and business plans, or lacking the courage to make necessary moves to actualize their ideas.

However on a positive note, I also came across many successful businesses started by people who gave birth to viable business ideas and nurtured them. They stuck to their business plans and pursued their dreams. When faced with challenges and the ever changing business environment, e.g. new information on business policy change, unforeseen circumstances, they adjusted accordingly - in other words they adapted to change and never gave up. This then enabled them to build very successful businesses.

As we have seen here the difference between being successful and not being successful is taking the appropriate action, and following it through without ever giving up on your dream. This kind of attitude also proves that persistence and determination are vital ingredients to success.

What is stopping you?

I once delivered an entrepreneurship workshop to a group of women in London who wanted to start a health care agency business. They had the relevant expertise, financial capital, and local knowledge. However, when I asked them at the start of the workshop what was holding them back, they gave a whole range of reasons as to why they had not taken the next step with their ideas.

Some of the reasons they gave was fear of failing, fear of the unknown, and lack of courage and confidence to move to the next level. However, two years after taking my start-up training course and coaching them, some are now running their own businesses. Sometimes all that one needs to get started is for someone to show them the way and believe in them.

People come up with business ideas all the time, but many of them never take off for various reasons, among the top reasons is fear and procrastination.

Fear and procrastination are the biggest enemies within ourselves. Inside everyone of us, there is a procrastinator - it feeds our mind with doubt, it keeps convincing us to put off doing things, thereby making it harder to get going. That procrastinating voice tries to convince us that now is not the right time to start, and that we need to wait for a certain time or condition to get started.

It is important to be aware of this procrastinator, as it can be full of creative and convincing excuses, giving us facts and alternative ideas that try and convince us why we should not take action now. As a result, we then find ourselves involved in activities that just waste our valuable time.

Like everything else, when thinking of taking your idea to the next level, be aware of that negative inner voice. Do not feed it, as it has a tendency of taking control if you allow it to grow and become stronger. There are also external procrastinators. These are the negative people who will not see the positive aspects of your idea. They will discourage you and be cold to your idea, these are the doubting Thomas.

You must therefore be alert and take control of your ideas and your mind especially in the early stages of incubating your ideas.

As we have seen above, the first obstructions you will face will be found within yourself. Allow yourself to feel the fear if you must, but shake it off, go ahead, and just do it anyway! It is better to fail trying, than to fail in life having not tried.

Good or bad idea?

There have been many instances when people have made harsh judgements on what they felt were bad business ideas, only for them to be proved wrong. During several episodes of the UK television programme *Dragons Den*, I watched some contestants who pitched their ideas, and were told by the dragon investors that they were not viable or not good enough businesses to be invested in, only for them to later turn out to be successful businesses. While the dragons saw and heard the business pitching and were only interested in what-is-in-it for them, what they overlooked was the hunger to succeed, the passion and the determination by some of the entrepreneurs.

The above dragon's scenarios therefore means if you have several business ideas, it is advisable to choose a business idea that you are passionate about and one that suits your style.
The more you love the type of business you are going into, the more fulfilled you will feel, and the more likely you are to succeed. It is best not to go into a business purely for financial reasons as you also want to enjoy what you will be doing – this is often the best motivator for success and fulfillment. Sometimes being rejected can give some people the extra determination they need to prove the doubters wrong, therefore when people reject your viable business idea, do not be discouraged but follow your passion always.

As a business portfolio manager for a major bank in London, I listened to many ideas pitched to me by those seeking start-up packages. Some of the ideas sounded ridiculous to me at the time, however, I sometimes witnessed what seemed like ridiculous ideas take off and become profitable, sustainable businesses.

Technically speaking then, there is no such thing as a good or bad business idea, rather, it is good business execution, passion, determination, and the focus involved in carrying out the work that matters the most.

In the following chapters we shall take a look at some of the most important strategies and things you can adopt, to turn your ideas into your business success story.

You have a business idea; should you share it?

So you have this wonderful and exciting business idea, what next? When it comes to sharing your ideas, there are two schools of thought.

1.   Some people feel it is a bad idea to share your business idea.

2.   Some think it is a good idea to share your business idea.

Let's have a look at both of these in more detail:
Those who follow the first school of thought and believe that sharing their idea, is in itself a bad idea, sometimes do so for good reasons.

It is true that ideas can get stolen. There have been cases where owners of original ideas have gone to court because they believed that their ideas had been stolen, or that they had been circumvented in some way. For example, I have read of cases where companies

7

sued each other for stealing logos or for having similar designs. If you come up with original ideas, then you have the right to safeguard those ideas. This is referred to as intellectual property rights, which are legally recognised rights to individual ideas and creations. Certain exclusive rights to intangible assets are granted under this law such as inventions, words, music, designs, symbols, literary and artistic works. If you are therefore worried that your original idea may be stolen, it is a good idea to seek protection of your idea or creation under this law.

There are also people who do not like to share ideas for fear of getting negative and unhelpful feedback, which they fear may kill their spirit, discourage them, or even slow down their start-up momentum.

Others may want to avoid frequent follow up questions on how their business idea is unfolding or how far they have gone with their idea from curious people. So to avoid the questions and curiosity from others, they prefer to mainly focus on what they want to achieve but they don't talk much about it to other people.

This first school of thought approach has worked for some people who have gone on to create successful businesses, but is it the best approach?

So let's now look at the second school of thought.

Sharing your idea has many benefits. In most situations the best advice is to share your idea with trusted family members, friends and colleagues, and ask for their feedback.
This will be beneficial as you should get constructive feedback that will help your idea to take shape.

You should also get other helpful information that you may not have thought of before, and which may help in bringing your idea to life.

Sharing your idea can also open doors and connect you to business referrals, potential clients, investors, and other helpful people who will add value to your entrepreneurship journey.

So sharing your idea with the right people is not all bad as we have seen. You stand to benefit a lot from feedback that will help you improve and shape the development of your idea, moving from visualising it, to proactively making it happen, and turning it into a reality.

Some entrepreneurs even sell or exchange their ideas for money. A good example of this is where an entrepreneur has a viable idea, but not enough investment capital, so they decide to source for angel investors to pitch their idea to, and exchange part of their business for money.

So do not be afraid to share your idea or be worried about someone stealing your idea. In the worst case scenario even if they steal your idea, they will not steal your passion, your uniqueness, your vision, your motivation, or your expertise. After all, ideas are in huge supply everywhere and are manufactured every day. Looking at it from a different perspective, there are so many businesses out there conducting similar businesses and they all have their dedicated clientele.

Business ideas are done in dozens, what really matters is that you take action and implement your idea. What makes your business unique is your Unique Selling Point (USP). This differentiating factor will make your business stand out and be known.

If however you really do feel that your idea may be at risk of being stolen or exploited, as mentioned on page 8, you may seek to copyright your idea through the appropriate channels in your country.

Existing ideas & businesses

Sometimes you do not need a new idea to get started. Some businesses have been built from other existing similar business ideas, and have gone on to be very successful. They do this by finding what other businesses are not doing well and why; what their customers are most unhappy and dissatisfied with; and then set about formulating solutions that solve the customers' problems.
They also figure out ways to do it better or differently from their competitors, or to just add better value to attract more customers.

If you look at big brands, banks or even supermarkets in your locality you will note that each one is known for its uniqueness. For example, all of my local supermarkets offer home deliveries, but some of them promise to unpack and put your shopping in the fridge for you. That is their USP on home deliveries, compared to the rest who will just leave your shopping at the door.

Write it down!

It may seem obvious but writing things down is good practice and in some cases very important and critical, as it helps you to remember everything you need to action. It can be a goal you need to achieve, things you must do, or a business idea you may have. Having goals and ideas written down will help you know when you have achieved progress, and you can celebrate your achievements.
Write your ideas on paper or use an electronic note taking or voice recording device. If your ideas are important to you, then they are worth recording.

If it is difficult to write all of your ideas down, then at least summarise them into a few pages, including all the most important aspects, and all the relevant questions you may have.
Writing your ideas down will give you clarity on the path you will need to take, and define the final desired outcome.

I have found that writing down my ideas and my desired goals always helps me to plan the best path to take in order to achieve my desired outcome. It also keeps me motivated to take action and remain focused. When you commit and write down what you need to do and how you want to do it, you will not get distracted as you will know the path you want to take.
Many great ideas are written down and that is as far as they go, they are just left there gathering dust. After writing down your ideas, the next step is to take the necessary action on them that will start the journey of fulfilling your dreams.

With the rising numbers of unemployed worldwide and if we have a desire to be financially independent and wealthy, then we must seek to understand Robert Kiyosaki cash-flow quadrant below. Being employed is not the best position in the quadrant. Taking your idea to the next level is the only way to climb up the tier.

EMPLOYED	BUSINESS OWNER
Have a job Exchanges time for money	Owns a system
SELF- EMPLOYED	INVESTOR
Owns a job. 95% Population 5 % Wealth	Own investments 5% Population 95% Wealth

Robert Kiyosaki Cash-flow Quadrant

SUMMARY

- *You have to believe in your idea and make it work.*

- *Have a clear vision of your business idea.*

- *Take action, don't just talk about it.*

- *Don't be afraid to fail as long as you learn from your mistakes.*

- *You are most likely to succeed when you enjoy what you do.*

- *Ambition is the first step to success. The second is action.*

Reflections

"If you've failed, that means you're doing something. If you're doing something, you have a chance."

Robert Kiyosaki

CHAPTER TWO

SET YOUR GOALS

Why do you need to set goals?

Successful entrepreneurs create systems and plans that remind them of how they will move from where they are, to where they need to be, in order to achieve success.

Goals set properly, will help you to progress your business in the right direction. In order to set workable goals, you have to know what you are working towards, be it in business or other areas of your life.

Setting your financial, personal, or business goals will help you to control the direction you want to take, and define the things that you need to know and understand, in order to achieve your desired outcomes. When you set goals for your business, make sure they are goals that will motivate you to do better and steer your business towards your desired end result.

For example, if you set goals to lose weight, you need to plan how, when, and where you will do it. There may be things you will need to change in your lifestyle, and things you may need to get rid of, or do less of. The first thing you will need to do is assess your regular eating habits. You may decide to reduce fattening foods, and include more fruits and vegetables into your diet.

You may also look at introducing physical exercise, and plan when and where you will do this, how often and for how long. By doing this you are creating a plan, and the journey you will need to follow to achieve your desired outcome, which in this case is to get fitter and healthier.

The beauty of planning and designing how you will go about achieving your goals, is that once you create the framework, it becomes the foundation of everything you will need to do in your journey to a successful outcome. When embarking on your business journey, create a framework that will become the foundation of everything you do in your business.

Start by writing your goals down. Writing goals down will help to reinforce them in your mind, and you will also have a reference point in case you forget anything, as you seek to accomplish your desired outcome.

All successful people and high achievers set clear goals and follow them through to the end. When you set your business goals, it helps you to develop focus, purpose, direction, and it channels your energy towards your desired results.

I have found out that whenever I set a specific goal to achieve something, instead of spreading myself too thin by focusing on several goals at a time, I achieved success by concentrating on the most important goal at that particular time, and the one that will create the biggest impact in what I wanted to achieve first.

The best strategy is to prioritise what is most important in your entrepreneurship journey and what will give you the most impact.

Vague goals produce vague results

When you set your business or any other goals, be clear and specific by creating a clear detailed plan with all of the steps you will need to take to achieve your planned and desired outcome.

To motivate you further, it may also help to create a list of benefits that accomplishing your goals will bring to your life and your loved ones. Most importantly bear in mind that, **vague goals will produce vague results but specific goals will produce specific results.**

Identify sacrifices that have to be made

In the early days of setting up your business, you may need to sacrifice things, which may include giving up some of your favorite activities. Putting more hours into your business is necessary for it to succeed, especially at the start. This may well require that you make necessary adjustments to your social and family life, and change some of your habits.

In order to identify what you need to sacrifice, you must first undertake a lifestyle audit so that you can understand how you spend your time, money and other resources. From there you will have a clearer idea of what you need to give up, do less of, and more importantly, start doing more of.

If, for example, you spend a lot of time on social media just browsing and sharing your social life, then you may identify this as something you need to adjust, either by doing less of it, or changing how you use it. For example, you can chose to use the time you spend on your social media more effectively by creating an online awareness of your business, and share this with your friends instead. You can also decide to reduce the time you spend on social media and spend more time on your business development. This is a more productive way of utilising the time you spend online.

You also need to scrutinise how you are spending your money. If there is a *must have* designer outfit, or latest gadget you want to buy, before spending any money or getting into debt for it, pause and ask yourself a few questions, is it necessary? can I wait? because spending your money on trendy things and impulse buying will not help in growing your business. The money you save can be put to better use. It can be money you put aside for emergency use when the business is still picking up. It is important to learn the discipline of delaying things until your goals are met.

Here are some of the questions you can use to help you set your business goals:

- What are your business goals?

- When do you want to achieve your goals?

- How will achieving your goals benefit your business?

- What sacrifices will you need to make in your personal and family life?

SMART Goals:

For goals to be powerful they must be **S.M.A.R.T.**

- *Specific*

- *Measurable*

- *Attainable*

- *Relevant*

- *Time Bound.*

A S.M.A.R.T. Goal Daily Planner for Business and Life

by Tasha T.C. Cooper.

Your business goals must be SMART; they must be specific, clear and well defined. For example, if you want to start your business next year, do not just set your goal to start next year. Be specific about the month, and refine it further down to the specific date of that month.

By being specific with the start date, you will be able to know how you are progressing, and ultimately measure your success, because you have a target date to work with. If you are faced with delays as you approach your target date, you will be aware of this because you have specified the day to launch your business.

Where possible, you will make adjustments and catch up by putting other unproductive tasks to the side, as you concentrate on getting things ready for your start date.

Set yourself challenging yet attainable goals. It is important to make sure goals you set for yourself are attainable but challenging. If you set unattainable goals you will most likely get demoralized, frustrated, demotivated, and most likely give up. For example, if you set a start date for your business before all the planning and logistics are in place, it may have a negative impact on your customers or clients as you will not be ready for them. So set a start date that is timely, and one that won't rush or delay the launch of your business.

Be flexible

Set goals that are in harmony with what you want to achieve and the direction you want your business to go. As you go along keep comparing notes with where you are now and how your business is unfolding. Tweak things as you go along if they need tweaking.

Many situations are fluid and you may find that you need to be flexible in some instances to achieve your goals.
In addition to your business goals, make it a habit to set goals in other areas of your life. Encourage those around you to get into the habit of setting goals, especially those you may be working with in your business. This will not only help others, but will also help you get into the habit of setting continuous goals.

Finally, to avoid obstacles that you may face, focus on your set goals and do not take your eyes off them. You might find it helpful to get yourself into rituals of thinking and talking positively about your goals.

Crystallize the success you want in your mind by visualizing it. The more you do this, the more you will attain the clarity to determine what you must do for your goals to become successful.

SUMMARY

Answer the following questions to help you set your goals;

- *What is your goal?*

- *How will you know when you achieve your goals?*

- *How will achieving your goals benefit you and others?*

- *When do you want to achieve your goals?*

- *Set goals that are in harmony with what you want to achieve.*

- *Put your set goals in writing and make them S.M.A.R.T.*
    - o Specific
    - o Measurable
    - o Attainable
    - o Relevant
    - o Time Bound

Reflections

CHAPTER THREE

PLANNING AND ORGANISING

Why you must plan

When starting your entrepreneurship journey, you will have many tasks. These can become a huge burden. Your performance and morale will be affected if you do not plan how things will be done, when they will be done, and by whom.

It is important to plan ahead. Plan for success, plan for failure, and for the mistakes you will make as you grow your business. Rushing at the last minute is not a good option. Plan and organize in advance. This will save you time and money.

Many entrepreneurs plan every detail of their business before they start. They adopt strategies and put systems in place that have made them successful in running very profitable businesses. We have all heard or known of businesses that have been passed on from one generation to another. Some of the secrets to the success of these businesses are, planning, putting systems in place and adopting strategies that have proved successful over the years.

For some start up businesses, it is not always possible to acquire all the resources and equipment needed to start. They know what they need to run their businesses smoothly but they may not be able to afford it. They start with what they have until their businesses pick up, and implement thing as they go along.

If you find yourself in this kind of situation, it should not deter you from starting. Get started with what you have, then plan to put systems in place as your business grows.

Let's next look at some important things you need to plan to help you in your entrepreneurship journey.

Planning

It is said, "Failing to plan is planning to fail." Without a clear plan you will find that you will be very busy running around doing a lot of work but not doing much in terms of productivity and achieving your goals. A clear organized plan will help you to avoid repetition of activities which are not fruitful. It will also help your business move forward by concentrating and doing more of those tasks that add value to your business objectives.

To start planning, look where you are now and where you want to be in the future with your business, and then put in place a long term strategic objective. Plan what you want to do, what you want to achieve, and how you will achieve it.

As we saw in chapter 1, the number one mistake procrastinators make is the lack of a plan to work with. This is a huge mistake as it makes them postpone starting or even accomplishing their goals. You will find that if you get into the habit of planning, organising, and diarising your activities according to priority, then these simple actions will keep you focused on your goals.

When I worked as a business manager in my previous banking career, I managed a large portfolio of clients. Planning my time was therefore essential in order to achieve my set targets. I found that when I used my diary and prioritised my activities, it really helped me to work seamlessly and remain focused, despite the high workload. I never needed to work extra time in the evening or weekend in order to catch up and meet my deadlines, as I prioritised and dealt with what was urgent first and got it out of the way.

Whenever I had a heavy work load or tight deadline, I delegated some of the work to other specialists. For example, if a client phoned me just to ask queries or make a complaint, I made sure that I addressed their issues by telephone through a dedicated customer services department. I recorded voice mail message informing my clients calling my line with queries or complaints that an alternative and faster ways of resolving their concerns was available. I thereafter diverted my phone to customer services, so that when my customers were talking to customer service they were aware through my recorded message that I was not available and that they will still get good service.

This in effect freed up my valuable time and I was able to concentrate on high value clients who would bring in lots of business.

I choose to work smart by using all of the tools and services available to me in order to achieve my set targets.

Plan to continually raise the bar by adopting best practices and methods. Maximize your time by working smarter and using technology to help you operate your business effectively and efficiently.

Business plan

Every business must have a business plan, however simple it may be. A business plan is helpful to investors and lenders in case you are planning to borrow money for your business. But it is not just for securing funding from lenders. It is your road map, and will help you understand and manage your business more effectively.

When you write your business plan and put your thoughts down, it gives you clarity to understand your business, the market place, your competitors, potential customers, suppliers, and the general environment you are getting into a little better.

With this knowledge you can then put a suitable workable strategy in place that will ensure you successfully operate within this environment. It is therefore essential to have a business plan as part of your planning, as it shows you the road you will need to travel to achieve success.

Marketing plan

There is a lot of noise out there in the market place and your visibility, or lack of it, will determine your success or failure. Putting a marketing plan in place before you get started is essential.

It will help you focus on your target market and remind you of the actions you will need to take to achieve the marketing goals of your business. A marketing plan will clearly spell out the vision and strategy you will use, and the tactics you will apply to get there. It will communicate to your target market who you are and what you do.

Conducting a S.W.O.T. and P.E.S.T. analysis will help you know the internal and external factors that can affect your business. (More about S.W.O.T. and P.E.S.T. analysis is covered in chapter 5). You need to ask yourself what you need to do to get noticed? Try and come up with creative solutions on how you will stand out from the crowd. Look at the channels that you have at your disposal that can help you stand out at low cost.

You do not want to spend a huge amount of money putting up adverts on TV or newspapers. Start small and start with what you have. Social Media platforms, blogs, Facebook, Twitter, Periscope, Instagram, and podcasts are good starting places to promote your business and/or expertise for free.

The best time to do marketing is not when you are desperate or when you have already started your business. You need to start promoting and advertising your business before hand. Also, do not stop promoting your brand after you start to become well known. A big and well known brand like Coca-Cola, spends millions in advertising non stop. They also re-brand themselves from time to time. Think of a well known brand and study how it has evolved over time, and the strategies used to stay relevant to the current business environment.

Remember attention is the new currency, and you need to capture the attention of your target market, constantly reminding them you are still in business or are going to start soon. They need to know your business is starting up soon even before you launch, so build that anticipation by letting them know the projected launch date, and what you will be offering.

Finances

Finances are the core of your business, it is therefore imperative to get them in order. Plan for them ahead of time and know where your start-up capital will come from.

Put systems in place that will manage your finances if you are going to do the book keeping. This will ensure that when invoices and receipts come in, they are processed without delay. The last thing you want is to be overwhelmed with lots of paper-work lying around unprocessed and without a system in which to process it. If you are going to hire an accountant to do your accounting, plan this in advance and agree on a fee.

If you predict that your business will grow beyond the VAT thresholds, it may be important to factor this in right from the start, and carry out the necessary registration, or seek advice on how to go about it.

It is imperative to separate your personal finances from your business finances in order to make it easier when you carry out your financial returns, and also to help you know how your business is doing financially. You will need a dedicated business account. Plan this ahead of time.

Take time to find out which financial institution is offering the best and most cost effective deal, as most banks will have different propositions and charges for their business accounts. Find out about how you should operate the account as in most cases, a business account has different terms and conditions to personal account.

When you are starting, it is important to keep your running costs as low as possible.

One way to achieve this is to learn some basic bookkeeping skills so that you can do the simple stuff yourself, and only engage an accountant with the more complex accounting bits.

Prioritising

If you are going to be a sole trader, you will likely be doing all of the work yourself. You will need to establish when things need to be done, record each activity in your diary according to priorities, and tick off things on your to-do-list as you complete them.
If you are going to employ people, every one of them must be clear on their shared responsibilities, and the work expected of them.
Set out clear priorities for them - what needs doing and by who, and when it must be done by.

Make planning and prioritising important things in your business a habit and one of your goals. They both go hand in hand and will help you get closer to achieving success. Plan and attend to the most urgent and important tasks at hand.

Plan and focus on what is important to help you achieve your goals. This is one of the most productive habits you can adopt, as it helps you to eliminate activities that are time wasting and not essential.

Tax and compliance

The purpose of this section is to highlight some of the taxation and regulatory compliances you need to check in order to ensure that your business is following the law.

There are statutory regulatory compliances and laws governing most businesses that must be adhered to. Find out about all the legal formalities you require for the type of business and entity you want to engage in.

Ask yourself, is it a regulated industry that your business is venturing into? If it is, it is a good idea to seek professional legal advice so as to remain compliant and avoid fines and penalties.

If you are not conversant with, or do not have the time to deal with some or all of the compliance issues such as taxes, stamp duty, Value Added Tax (VAT), then it might be a good thing to engage a qualified person such as an accountant. For complex legal matters and advise, it is important to seek the services of a qualified lawyer.

To ensure you do not incur losses in case of accident or penalties for non compliance, business insurance is an area you need to plan for in advance.

Here are some examples of business related insurances.

- Insuring against risks and liabilities.

- Employers limited cover.

- Public liability cover.

- Professional Indemnity cover.

- Income protection cover.

31

Trading formats

When setting up a business you will have to decide which trading structure is most appropriate for you and your business. The trading structure you choose will have implications on many aspects of your business. It affects your ability to raise finances, and some may impact on your personal liability, or even how your taxes are treated, among many other things.

If you are not sure which way to go, always seek professional advice from a qualified accountant or legal adviser.

Examples of some of the business structures that exist:

- Sole trader.

- Partnership, e.g. 50/50.

- Limited Liability Partnership.

- Private limited Company.

- Company Limited by Guarantee.

- Social Enterprise structure.

- Franchise.

After all the planning and prioritising is done, it is important to stick to the plan, but also be prepared to be flexible where necessary. For example, you may come across something which requires you do things in a different way, and this means you need to be willing to be flexible. Things can change, and it is important to bear that in mind, so leave room for flexibility, and adapt to change as it happens.

SUMMARY

- *A written plan is your road map that will lead you to your destiny.*

- *A written plan will help you know when you are on track.*

- *A written plan will help potential investors see your plans and invest in you.*

- *A written plan will guide your mentors to give you additional direction.*

•

"

Failing to plan is planning to fail

"

- Allen Lakein

Reflections

CHAPTER
FOUR

BUSINESS AND NON-BUSINESS CONSIDERATIONS

Is Work-life-balance important?

When growing up in a household of entrepreneurs, I learnt early in life that what they today call "work-life-balance" is something of a myth when it comes to running your own business.

Any entrepreneur will tell you that one of their biggest challenges after starting their business is determining how to harmoniously integrate their business and personal lives and get a good balance.

You might find that most of your time is dedicated to your business, especially in the early stages. However, if you work too hard, your health, and even your relationships, could suffer. Likewise, if you focus too much on your personal life, you stand to lose your competitive edge with the business.

So how do you find the right work life balance? Work life balance is rarely achieved, and it is up to you as an entrepreneur to figure out what balance works best for your business and personal life.

It is therefore very important to have this discussion with your family and close friends so that you can get their moral and practical support. When you have their understanding, it will become a team effort, instead of having to struggle alone trying to balance things out.

Personal finance

While some entrepreneurs prefer to raise capital through borrowing, some prefer to go it alone and fund their businesses from their own personal finances. There are of course pros and cons of using personal finances to fund your business as we shall see in the rest of the book.

Once you get funding for your business (as detailed in Chapter 3), do not put it all together with your personal money. It should be held in a separate dedicated business account. This will make your work easier when doing your tax returns or auditing.

During my time as a business advisor, I came across many businesses that were self funded. Some of my clients were eligible for funding but they opted not to borrow. Reasons were varied as to why they preferred self funding. Some wanted to ensure full control of how they ran their business and not be accountable to lenders.

Others did not like the idea of giving their assets as security for their borrowing, which for some involved releasing equity on their home. For some, going it alone was the only option they had, as they were not eligible for funding. Some intentionally avoided borrowing as they did not want the cost of debt to eat into their profits.

These real world examples are all valid reasons to fund your own business if you can afford to, or if your circumstances do not allow for borrowing. However you do need to bear in mind that going this route may affect your standard of living, and put a strain on your personal budget if you are already having to make sacrifices. It also increases personal risk if the business fails. Although, on the positive side, it is good to avoid debt in the early stages of starting if you can afford to, as borrowing can be expensive, and there is no guarantee that your business will make enough money in the early stages to pay back loans.

You therefore need to plan and budget carefully if you are going to self fund. Plan how much of your personal finances you are prepared to put into the business and stick to that plan by writing down your own *survival budget* as shown in chapter 7. Do not get tempted to keep putting more and more of your personal finances into the business if it is not achieving the desired results.

Work place issues

With today's technology, and the internet widely available, it is possible to work from almost anywhere. You can stay in touch with clients, co-workers, and bosses, quite easily, by using such things as email, social media, and electronic conference applications.
If for example, you are selling goods, you do not necessarily need a commercial shop, as you have the option to do business on the internet. Online stores are the future as they help reduce operating expenses by eliminating the need for commercial premises. Amazon, E-bay, Alibaba, to mention just a few, are all online businesses that are very successful. I myself am using Amazon as one of the channels to sell this book online, and you too can partner with some of these companies to sell your goods.
You can also create your own website, use social media, affiliate to online stores, or use any combination of these.

The idea here is to cut your operation costs by looking at the most cost effective options available when you are starting.

In some cases you can swap between two working venues, where you can work from home, but from time to time you might need an office space for meetings or interviews – in which case you can look at hiring temporary office space, known as smart offices.
This could save your business money as you will not have the commitment of monthly or annual rental charges.
Given that you can save a lot of money going this route, you should therefore consider working from home and hiring office space, exhibition stores etc as and when you need to, as commercial premises increase your operating costs and eat into your profits.

There are some cases where you can only work from a commercial premises due to nature of the business and in this case you must have a physical business premises. You will therefore need to plan the most suitable location for your business, be it a shop, an office or a warehouse.

There are many options out there, and depending on the nature of your business you need to choose what is suitable for the kinds of products and services you are offering.

Working from home

If you are going to work from home, or are already working from home, make sure your business is not restricted to run from home. Get all the necessary permissions and give the required notification to your landlord or local authority as the case may be.

Another important thing to check is that any legal agreements you have signed with regard to mortgage, insurance, lease or rental contracts, allows you to work from home. If you are not sure seek advice so that you do not find yourself or your business in trouble.

Check the practical issues of working from home. If you are dealing with customers on a regular basis, then for your own privacy and security it may not be the best idea to work from home.

You should also consider security and/or insurance for any stock or equipment that you hold at home, so make sure you have adequate cover.

Another issue you may need to consider is how easy it would be to work from home without distractions, or people who may seek your attention.

If you are working from home, you may also wish to check if you can claim back some bills such as electricity, and part of your mortgage or rent as a tax allowance. You can liaise with your accountant or seek professional advice if you are not sure how to go about claiming back work related expenses.

Finally, protect what is important to you, that is, your assets by ensuring that you have adequate insurance protection cover for your home, business, yourself and your family.

Putting into consideration all important non-business related issues will help you to determine how to harmoniously integrate your business and personal life, in order to achieve a good work-life-balance to productivity ratio. This will ultimately help you to create your ideal lifestyle along with a successful business.

SUMMARY

- *Find a work- life- balance that work for you.*

- *Protect your assets, wealth, health and whatever else is important to you.*

- *Separate personal and business finances. Maintain separate accounts.*

- *Leverage on technology to get your ideal work life balance.*

"Give me six hours to chop down a tree, and I will spend the first four sharpening the axe"

- Abraham Lincoln

Reflections

CHAPTER
FIVE

IDENTIFY AND UNDERSTAND YOUR BUSINESS NICHE

In the initial stages of starting your business, you are bound to succeed if you arm your business with as much information and data on your target market as possible!

What you are offering may not be suitable for everyone, therefore it is vital to have a well defined market as you will find it difficult to sell it to everyone. By targeting a niche market you stand a good chance to compete with the best and largest in the market place.

In this chapter we will look at some of the things you can do to effectively research and understand more about your target market, your competitors, and your potential customers. Researching your business niche will arm you with vital information that will help you stand out in the market place.

Before I started doing my market research for my training workshops and coaching, I armed myself with a list of my desired target market and ideal clients. The next thing I wanted to find out was where these clients could be found so that I could communicate with them about my training workshops and coaching programs.

Before embarking on your research journey, first make a list of all the things you want to know more about and research on. You need to determine what information you need, and what problems and issues need to be addressed.

What should you research?

The following list will give you some ideas of the things you can research.

- Customers and Markets.

- Competition and price.

- Business & Marketing plan.

- Trading Formats.

- Compliance.

- Costs.

Why you need target market research

In most areas of life knowledge is power. This is especially true in business. The more knowledge you have, the better prepared you will be to succeed. As entrepreneurs, we all have these great ideas, and although the thought of starting a new business is very exciting, it is very important to first check and test if your ideas will have a sufficient demand in the market place before jumping in. Before you launch your business, you need to get as much information about your target market as you can.

Researching your market will help you find out and understand how the industry you are about to venture into has performed in the past, and what is coming in the future. It can be the difference between a successful thriving business and an expensive failure. To set up a successful business, you will need to get out of your comfort zone and talk to people.

Remember the customer is king, and researching your market will help you understand what your potential customers really need and want, where and how they want it, who they currently get it from, and how much they are willing to pay for it.

With that information you can then refine your product or service and tailor them to meet your customers needs, before committing yourself to expensive product development costs.

You will also learn more about your competitors and what they offer, which should give you a competitive advantage.

How to do your research

Let's look at some of the things you can do to research your market. Before I ventured out into my training and coaching business, empowering women and young people in Africa and the United Kingdom, I first researched where my clients are found, how I would reach out to them and in some cases, it meant travelling between the two continents to gather all the information I needed before launching my business.

I wanted to know what my potential clients needs are, so I did several free training to test the market and get feedback. In addition, I did my research on who else was doing the same business in the geographical areas I wanted to target. I also did a few presentations in partnership with those who are in the same field. This gave my business mileage as many in attendance got to know about me and my business. Through referral, I have since been invited to several business conference events to present and empower delegates.

Sometimes you need to go out of your way and comfort zone to get vital information in order to strategize effectively.

First, identify your market and ask yourself what market segment you will be targeting, whether it be the whole market or a specific part of it. You can then narrow down to the specific section you want to target in order to develop your marketing strategy.

Primary and secondary research

In your research you can use primary and secondary research to get the information you need. Primary being the new research you will carry out by asking specific questions through various methodologies, for example, you can decide to use questionnaires.

You can also combine your research with secondary research, which has been previously researched for other purposes, and is readily available for public use. Libraries, private businesses, and government agencies that are in your areas of interest can give you valuable information that is readily available.

Networking and talking to people

It is said that your network is your net worth. Networking with likeminded people is one of my favourite activities. I always make sure I google and facebook meet-up events of the areas I am interested in, whether in London or other cities I frequently visit.

Through these networking events, and various other, I have created and continue to create, my business networks.
There are always some networking events going in a city near you, if you take the time to look on the internet you will find events of interest. I have always found this to be a great way of meeting new people with mutual interests and learning new ways of doing things through interacting with them.
Try and make it a point (if you are not already doing so) to attend business and social networking events of interest, where you can meet and network with new people, learn new things, and get business leads.

You can also talk to the industry experts so that you have a better understanding of whether your business idea is feasible. In addition to this, there should also be a wealth of information available to the public on every industry sector in most countries, which should provide information about how a particular sector has performed in the past, how it is currently performing, and other helpful information - find out the relevant government body for your country that can give you this information.

Volunteering

Another great thing you can do is to volunteer to work in the industry you are interested in. You will learn so much about how it works and discover new things that you may not have known before. Many organizations seek volunteers, either on part-time or full time basis and are willing to exchange or offer free training for your time. You will gain a lot of experience in various area, technical and practical skills that are not taught in college and life skills e.g team work, time keeping skills, working under pressure and tight deadlines are all skills and experience that you may find helpful in your own venture. You will learn valuable lessons as you give your time.

Get to know your potential customers

One of the most important things you will need to do is identify your niche market, and the more specific you are the better. Do not just market to everyone. For example, if you want to target your product or service to the younger millennial generation, you need to first find out the best way to reach out to them. If, let's say, you decided to put an advertisement in a newspaper to target this niche, you may find you are only reaching out to the older generation, who will most likely buy and read newspapers. Your intended target audience in this case is the younger generation, who are less likely to buy or read newspapers and more likely to be online. Therefore a better way to reach young people might be to advertise on social media and other online platforms where they are likely to have more presence.
It is therefore important to research and get to know your potential customers, know what they want, understand how you can communicate to and with them, what they look like, their ages, gender, social class, income, where they live, what price they are willing to pay for what you are offering, the level of quality and service they want, their buying habits and where and from who they currently buy from. This will help you offer them what they want.

As we have seen, determining how you will communicate with your niche and what methods you will use is therefore very important as you do not want to waste your valuable time and money just advertising to anyone and everyone. Offering your customer what

they want will be of mutual benefit as you will make them satisfied by offering value and what they want, this in return will keep them coming for more as you reap the benefits of repeat business and referrals.

If you have a prototype of your product, you can also test it on a few potential customers by offering them a sample product for free, and then get their feedback about what they think of it. This will help you to get inside your customer's head, and get to know what they really want and need. Based on their feedback, you can then tweak your product accordingly.

Research your competitors

You want to find out as much information as you can about your competitors so that you can use that information to develop your competitive edge. Find out who they are, where they are located, what they are offering and at what price, their successes and failures, and other important things.

If there are many competitors, it doesn't mean there is no market for you, so do not be worried about competition. Instead, look at it from a positive point of view – if there is a lot of competition, it means there is a lot of demand for the products or services that you offer.

In order to beat competition, you need to differentiate your product or service by adding extra value that addresses customers needs, and stands out from what others are offering. Another way to stand out from the competition is by branding your business, product, or service, in a new and unique way.

Competition is not always a bad thing.

Sometimes having a competitor is not always bad news, there are times people and businesses can work with a competitor to achieve a certain result. Sometimes collaborating with competitors can be of mutual benefit. Example of this is where musicians collaborate with one another to perform in a gig or make a record. Businesses sometime form consortiums and collaborations for mutual benefit, for example, a business may have the experience and another may have the finances. They then decide to leverage on what each has for mutual benefit.

Pricing

Some businesses try to compete with others based on price, however it is important to understand that no matter how cheap you charge, there will always be someone who cannot afford it, and no matter how expensive your price is, there will always be someone who can afford it. Instead of differentiating yourself with price, use other factors to stand out, for example, your positioning, branding, expertise, marketing strategy to differentiate your business from everybody else.

Use PEST and SWOT Analysis

P.E.S.T. is an acronym for Political, Economic, Social and Technological factors.

It looks at external opportunities and threats and should be part of your market research, as it will help to ensure that you don't overlook any important external factors.

Political changes can sometimes affect your business through new government policies. Economic changes such as interest rates and inflation all affect businesses. Social changes such as trends and population growth are all important to understand when in you are in business. Equally important are technological changes such as new computer technology and software, and automation processes.

S.W.O.T. is an acronym for Strengths, Weaknesses, Opportunities, and Threats. Strengths and weaknesses are internal to your business. Strengths are about the advantage you have over competition or all the good things you are good at, such as the experience and/or qualifications you have.

Weaknesses on the other hand are where you or your business have areas that need developing, for example, your sales technique if you don't have sales experience.

Opportunities and threats relates to the wider marketplace that your business operates and competes in. For example, a new transport link can be an opportunity to link your area to other cities opening up new opportunities for you there. Threats can for example come in the form of government regulations for the industry you are in.

You can do a S.W.O.T. analysis on your competitors and yourself. This will help you to analyse and understand your competitors and your own strengths and weaknesses. By doing this analysis, you will be able to identify the opportunities and threats your business faces and identify ways to overcome challenges.

By looking at yourself and your competitors using the S.W.O.T, you can begin to build a strategy to help you successfully position yourself in your target market.

The Internet

The internet is a powerful research tool. It has a wealth of information that you can gather in any field by spending just a few hours online. You can do a lot of very quick, effective researches on the internet, looking at who your potential competitors are. You can also do online surveys by posting questionnaires on social media or through email.

Money

As well as being well informed about your competitors, you also need to know how much money you need to get started, and where the money will come from. Make a list of all the resources you have and what you need to buy. Research where you can get what you need at the price you can afford.

More importantly, get to know the right time to buy things at low prices. Here is an example of what I learned when I was growing up: My parents ran a wholesale shop, amongst other businesses. During harvest season they would buy newly harvested cereals in bulk and keep them in a warehouse. Buying during this season when the demand was low meant they were able to buy it at a lower price. They would later sell the same cereals in a different season when the supply was lower and demand was high, and made a significant profit.

From my parents' way of transacting this cereal business, I learned the secret of leveraging on different seasons to buy low and sell high to make a profit. Timing is everything, and you can save and make money by transacting at the right time. Do your research and get a good understanding of how and when to make purchases for your business.

Breaking-even

When selling your products or services, you need to factor in all incurred costs, and quantify the time incurred, as you will need these when calculating your break-even point.
If you carry out initial research on how much things cost to buy and sell, this will help you understand at what point you will break-even, and at what point you will start to make a profit.

When you have worked out the price you need to sell at to break even, you can also look at other factors that can help you maximize your profits, for instance you can look into your operational costs, and find out if there is any unnecessary cost you can get rid of. In chapter 7 you will find more details on how to calculate your break-even point.

What is the best route to the market?

It is important to conduct research on how you will enter the market and the marketing channels you are going to use. After you have done your market research and gathered all the relevant information you will need, do not leave this information to gather dust. Act on it now because you will have a better understanding of your target market and your competitors.

With this information you can create a business strategy that will successfully work for you and your business, and define your Unique Selling Proposition (U.S.P). It will enable your 'brand' to stand out as a unique product or service that people will want to buy, as you meet their needs and desires.

SUMMARY

- *Market research will help you in creating the strategy that will work for you and your business.*

- *Understand your industry inside and out.*

- *Research your idea-*
  is it feasible, is it viable, is it sustainable?

- *Know who your customers are.*

- *Looking at yourself and your competitors using the SWOT framework.*

Reflections

CHAPTER
SIX

TEST YOUR MARKET

Before spending a lot of time and money developing your business product or service, it is important to establish that there will be sufficient demand for it by testing it first.

Many would-be entrepreneurs fail because they venture into a business based on what they think people want to buy, rather than what people do actually want to buy. This is one of the biggest mistakes one can make, as many businesses fail for this reason alone. You will need to arm yourself with other vital information, including what the customer really wants, how they want it and at what price they are willing to buy.

Testing the market before you launch your business can give you a big advantage in the marketplace. You will find out many things that will give you a competitive advantage, for instance, you will know if there is sufficient demand for your product or service, and if there is likely to be a growing or declining need for it, amongst other things.

The information you will gather whilst testing the market, will help you tweak and position your product or service according to the information you receive. This will make it more appealing to your customers' needs and wants.

In the rest of the chapter we shall look at some of things you can do to confirm if your product or service is something that is needed before you launch it.

Build a prototype or test the service

A sample of what you intend to launch is a good way to test the market. Family, friends, colleagues, online community focus groups can all be a good starting point to test your product or service, as these are the trusted people you can brainstorm with in a safe environment. They can also give you some good ideas that may help you to improve.

You can for example target a number of potential customers who can critically review what you are offering, and ask them to give you honest feedback. If there is a similar offer in the market place, ask them to compare it to your competitors product or service to see which one they prefer and why.

Honest feedback from people who do not like your product or service can help you refine and improve your offer. Equally, positive feedback will give you confirmation that your product or service is better than the competition, and therefore likely to succeed in the market place.

Use the internet

Use the internet to obtain the information you need that is relevant to the market for your product or service. This information should give you an indication of the demand for your product or service and how best to market it. Testing the market online also gives you limitless resources for trying out and testing your idea. You can use social media, online forums, Google keyword, Google insights, Google trends and countless other online platforms.
All of these will show you what people are searching for online, what is trending, and where these customers are located. You can also get more detailed information including the income, demography, age, gender, and how many customers are looking for the specific type of product or service that you offer. Just ask Google and you will find sites that will help you with this.

Your test market is valuable

Big companies spend a lot of resources measuring and testing demand through advertising and hiring people, before launching their product or service. This same test markets turns out to be their customers and advocates for their products and services. You can also in your small way, test the market, just like the big companies do.

You do not have to spend a lot of money as you can test your market with the contacts and networks you already have, and ask them for their feedback. These same people will spread the word as they test your products or services and bring in business for you by referring their family, friends, and colleagues These referrals may even turn out to be your long term customers if your business retains them and builds an ongoing relationship.

Start compiling a list of contacts and keep building them as you network and meet more potential customers. Your contacts list will turn out to be one of the most valuable assets you will ever have. If your business has a social media presence, ask these contacts to follow you so they can be updated whenever they check you out.

The next thing to do after building your contacts list is to start developing a communications strategy. This strategy will ensure that you keep in touch with all your potential customers on a regular basis.

Today there are many tools you can use to keep in touch with your contacts list, from emails, to forming groups on social media such as Facebook, Twitter, WhatsApp, Telegram, LinkedIn and so on.. You can create a group in any of the social media channels to keep your customers and potential customers in the loop and updated with your business developments.

Tweak it to suit your target market

After you have done the testing with your prototype, you will have learnt some new things that you can use to tweak and improve on your original ideas. Act on the interest shown by your test market and tailor your product or service in line with what your potential customers really want, and not what you thought they wanted.

SUMMARY

- *Build a prototype or test the service.*

- *Welcome both positive and negative feedback to improve.*

- *Tailor your products or services to your customers needs.*

- *Build a contact list from all those you are in contact in and keep them informed.*

Reflections

CHAPTER
SEVEN

MANAGING YOUR FINANCES

Numbers, accounts and finances, are some of my favourite topics, and I will therefore not finish this book without going through some of the financial aspects of running a business.

Some businesses prefer to outsource or delegate the most complex bits of financial accounting to a professional. There are various reasons why they do this. Some do this to leverage on time as they concentrate on other aspects of their business. For others, it is because they do not have the time to go through the complex process. For some, they would rather not do it at all but leave it to the experts. Whatever route you chose to follow, make sure your financial books and statements are always up to date.

That said, there is no harm in familiarising yourself with financial statements, or learning any other skills that you may find useful in running your business. In the rest of this chapter, we going to have a brief preview of some of the financial aspects that are important.

Financial overview

Financial statements communicate the state of affairs of your business, both currently, and in the past. They also give you an indication of how your business is doing compared to your goals and objectives.

Financial statements also act as indicators to investors of whether they should do business with you or not. Therefore every business that is planning to execute a sustainable business model must understand the importance of financial statements.

A good example of why it is important to maintain your financial statements is when it comes to borrowing for your business. Lenders will make their lending decisions based on financial statements, amongst other things. The state of your financial statements will guide them in deciding if they will lend to your business or not.

Financial statements are also helpful in dealing with government agencies and other stakeholders with regard to the amount of taxes, and V.A.T. payable to them, or in some cases refunds to your business.

The three most important and most common financial statements are, The Cash Flow Statement, The Profit and Loss Statement, and The Balance Sheet.

We shall now go through some of the basic statements and the calculations required, such as break-even point, return on investment, personal survival budget, cash flow and income and expenditure. All of these are quite straight forward and should help you in planning your business effectively.

It is important to familiarise yourself with financial statements even if you are outsourcing the accounting aspects of your business.

Where will the capital come from

It is very important to think carefully where your capital will come from, as it can have a great impact on your business. You may have been planning to save from your salary, or you may have a lump sum waiting to be put to good use. This is one of many sources of startup funding.

Family and friends are another source. They need to buy your idea first before they can be convinced that your idea can work. It is therefore a good idea to discuss with them in detail, your vision and how it is going to work, before asking for financial support.

There are also commercial lenders, but make sure you do your home work before settling for any lender. It is a good idea to shop around in order to see what each has to offer, as different institutions have different requirements for lending. Some lenders require security or guarantee, others may have higher charges and other fees, on top of interest to be paid back. You will need to compare to make sure you are not servicing an expensive loan while there are cheaper options available.

Investors may also be interested in investing in your business if you pitch a good idea to them, however, bear in mind that the amount they invest will determine the percentage of profits they take from your business, and they will have a say in how your business is run.There are many other sources of funding as shown in the next page. Go through each one of them and try to find out more about what is available in your local area.

Here are some common sources of funding:

Own Funds	• Savings • Salary
Family and Friends	• Gift • Loan
Borrow	• Commercial lenders - e.g. Banks, • Sacco's. • Credit Union - lend to members only. • Non Commercial lenders - e.g. Soft loans funds.
Investors (Equity Finance)	• Business Angels investor. • Venture Capitalists.
Grants & Bursaries	• Running Community Projects
Crowd funding	• Go Fund Me *There are many online fundraising platforms in different countries. e.g. M-changa in Kenya.*

Break - even point

Break-even point is reached when the total revenue exactly matches the total costs, and the business is not making a profit or a loss. In other words, it is the point of balance between making either a profit or a loss.

Establishing the break-even point helps to plan the number of units you need to sell in order to make profit, or at what price to sell the units at to be profitable.

Calculating profitability first involves working out the minimum level of sales required to cover all costs.

A loss is made when a business is not selling enough units for revenue to cover the costs. As more items are sold, the total revenue increases and covers more of the costs.
A profit is made when you sell above the break-even point.

In the next page we are going to look at a simple formula you can use to help you calculate your break-even point.

Information is power, and when you arm yourself with how much you need to sell and at what price in order to break-even, you will be working strategically with a purpose and target in mind, using the right strategies.

Calculating break - even point

Three figures have an impact on the breakeven point:

1. **Fixed cost/Overheads = Premises, Insurance, Permanent Employees.**

2. **Selling Price.**

3. **Variable cost/production cost per unit – e.g. casual labour.**

Let's look at an example of how to calculate the break-even point in order to know how many units need to be sold to break even.

Let's assume Mr. X is selling biscuits. How many biscuits does he need to sell to break even?

Fixed Cost = £25,000
SPU - Sales per unit = Selling price £1 per unit.
CPU - Cost per unit = Variable cost £0.50 per unit
BEP = break-even point.

Fixed Cost = BEP   £25,000.00 = 50,000 units.
(SPU-CPU)   (£1.00-£0.50)

Mr. X will need to sell **50,000** units to break even.

But If Mr. X wants to break-even earlier by selling less units, for

example, to sell 25,000 units instead of 50,000, what does he need to do?

He has a number of options as listed below:

1. He can raise the price.

2. Decrease his variable costs.

3. Use efficient ways of production.

4. Reduce number of employees.

5. Reduce fixed costs e.g. downsize office.

Return on Investment (ROI)

Return on investment (ROI) is a business term used to identify past and potential financial returns or in simple terms, it is cash on cash returns. ROI is a performance measure used to evaluate the efficiency of an investment, and is often expressed as a percentage or a ratio. This value can describe anything from a financial return to increased efficiencies.

Before venturing into business, it is worthwhile researching a few areas. Will it give you good returns for what you put in? The ROI formula helps you to understand if an investment is likely to have a positive ROI, or if there are other opportunities with a higher ROI, which should help you to determine the most lucrative opportunities.

To calculate ROI, the benefit (return) of an investment is divided by the cost of the investment; the result is expressed as a percentage or a ratio.

A high **ROI** means the potential gain of an investment compares favourably to the investment cost.

The return on investment basic formula:

ROI (%) = Net Profit/Total investment x 100

EXAMPLE: 1

John invests in £1,000 in Vodafone shares in 2016, in 2017 he sold his shares for a total of £1200. To calculate his ROI he will take his profit of (£1200-£1000=£200) and divide by investment cost £1000. £200/£1000x100= **20%**

EXAMPLE: 2

You purchase a property and put a down payment, and it generates a monthly income.

Purchase price £500,000

Down payment £ 100,000

Monthly income £2000

Your R.O.I. is £2000 x 12 months (Annual profit) = £24,000 divided by £100,000 (your down payment) = **24%**

Personal Survival Budget

When venturing into business it is important to know how much money you and your family will need to live on for the year, and to set that aside.

You can calculate this using a personal survival budget template. With a personal survival budget plan in place you can then allocate future personal income towards expenses, savings, and debt repayments.

Working out your personal survival budget helps you to work out your living costs for that period, it could be per month/year. This will help you to know how much money your business needs to make to cater for the money you will need to live on.

A good starting point with a personal survival budget is to find out how much you need to live on from your business in order to survive for the next 12 months? Each person's living costs may vary due to differences in commitments and lifestyles.

A personal survival budget can also help to raise finances from lending institutions. Before most lenders lend to you, they will want to know that you can afford to repay the loan.
They will therefore look into your finances, including the money you need to live on to determine your loan affordability.

If your personal survival budget shows that your business will make enough money for you to live on, and to pay back the loan, then you will stand a good chance of securing the loan. It is therefore important to put into account all your personal expenses, that is, the money you will need to live on to pay your personal bills and separate that from money you will need to run your business.

Personal Survival Budget Example Template

A	Estimate Expenditure for You & Family	Weekly	Monthly	Yearly
	Rent / Mortgage			£
	Utility bills			£
	Insurance - Personal/ Property			£
	Food & General Housekeeping			£
	Loan repayments/Credit Cards			
	Pension Contribution / Savings Plan			£
	School Fees			£
	Personal Expenses - Hobbies/Clothing/Holiday			£
	Car Expenses/ Maintenance			£
	Subtotal			£
	Contingency @ 5%			£
	Total Expenditure			£
B	**Estimated Income-Non Business**	Weekly	Monthly	Yearly
	Partner (Net Income)			£
	Employment			£
	Pension/Investments			£
	Other Income			£
	Total Income			£
	Survival Income required from business (A-B)			£

Cash Flow

The Cash Flow Statement is easy to do and can give you a quick snap shot of how cash is coming in and out of your business. It is something you should get into the habit of doing to get a feel for how your business is doing in terms of cash flow.

Cash is not the same thing as profit. You can have a profitable business but run out of cash. This is because cash comes in and out of the business at irregular intervals.

Commonly used terms in cash flow

Cash in - All income you expect to receive during the lifetime of your business. It can be calculated on a weekly, monthly, or yearly basis. e.g. grants, loans, shares, savings, own savings, sales.

Cash out - All business outgoings. Including overheads, purchase of equipment, stationery, advertising, and other associated costs.

Weekly/monthly balance - Cash in minus cash out = weekly balance.

Running/cumulative balance - Previous week/month balance plus current balance.

In a nutshell, this is what cash flow may mean to your business.

Cash going out is more than cash coming in	**Means Problems**
Cash going out equals cash coming in	**Not too bad (you are at breakeven point)**
Cash coming in is more than cash going out	**It's good News (you are in profit)**

Cash Flow Forecast Template

Week/Month	1	2	3	4	5
1. Cash In					
Grants/Loans					
Sales					
Total					
2. Cash Out					
Rent					
Equipment					
Material					
Wages					
Advertising					
Total					
3. Weekly/Monthly Balance					
4. Running Balance					

Income & Expenditure

Terms used in income and expenditure:

Income = money coming in.

Expenditure = money going out.

The income and expenditure statement, also known as the profit and loss account, is a record showing the amount of money coming into and going out of a business over a period of time (weekly, monthly, yearly).

It is important for you to keep a record of your Income (the money coming in) and your Expenditure (the money going out). This will help you to know how much money is in the business at any one time.

It's also important to track your expenditure for tax purposes, and to ensure that you only pay the amount of tax required.

Income & Expenditure - Sample Template

Business sales	£
Other Income A	£
Other income B	£
Total Income	£
Expenditure	
Paid by Cash	£
Rent & Rates	£
Utilities	£
Advertising	£
Insurance	£
Loan Repayment/Credit Cards	£
Depreciation	£
Total Expenditure	£

Reconciliation statement

You should make it a habit to reconcile your statements with your banking activities. That way you will verify that the transitions going through your accounts are valid. In case there are any unauthorised transactions, you will be able to track them quickly and resolve the issue as soon as possible.

There may also be times when charges or standing orders that were meant to be cancelled still go through, so regular checks of your statements should also help to spot these, and allow you to take the appropriate action.

Your reconciliation statement summarises your business and banking activities. It shows the withdrawals, deposits, and any other activities impacting your account for a specific period of time, helping you to keep track of your money.

Maintain and update your reconciliation statement regularly, as poor record keeping can result in paying high taxes and charges if you're unable to see exactly how much money is coming in and going out of your business.

Regular financial statement maintenance will help your business in budgeting and financial planning, and will play an important role in how your business is run. For the more complex statements, unless you have some fairly advanced accounting knowhow and the time to do it, it is best to outsource the work to a qualified accountant.

SUMMARY

- *Plan and manage both your personal and business finances separately, as it can have a great impact on your business.*

- *Financial statements act as indicators to others on whether they should do business with you or not.*

- *Lenders make their lending decisions based on the state of your financial statements.*

"If you don't control your money, making more won't help, you will just increase your expenditures"

Reflections

CHAPTER
EIGHT

SUCCESSFUL ENTREPRENEUR'S MINDSET

To be a successful entrepreneur, you do not necessarily need a first class degree from the most recognised university, but you do need to develop and cultivate a certain mindset to be successful in your business.

Some of the richest people within any given society are self employed or are involved in business ownership in some way, as we have seen demonstrated in Chapter One by the *Kiyosaki cash-flow quadrant*.

While some people will blame external factors for their failures, the smart and most successful people look within themselves for the reasons. In something called the 80/20 rule, 80% of the reasons that are holding people back are within themselves, and only 20% are external.

Successful entrepreneurs will seek to have a broad skill set that enables them to adapt to change. They have a thirst for learning new things and new ways of doing business, making them more productive and efficient.

There are many reasons why some people do not grow their businesses as much as they would like. One of the reasons is that the world is changing very fast, and to keep up, it is important to not get stuck in the old outmoded ways of running a business.

In your entrepreneurship journey you will always need to be self aware, internalize and look within yourself or your team to see where you might need to develop. It could be that you need to learn some new skills to run your business better, such as, computer or accounting skills, how to effectively use social media for business, selling skills, customer service, communication skills and the list is endless.

Learn to adapt to the times and learn new things to stay ahead of the curve. Make changes and adaptations where you must, mentally or physically, to help you adapt to the current business environment and remain competitive.

Therefore, before starting your business, it's important to internalise and ask yourself a few questions.

- What new skills are needed in this business?
- What is my competitive advantage?
- Why and how am I uniquely qualified to succeed in the business I am venturing into?
- What are my unique qualities or expertise that will ensure that my business succeeds?

Always prepared

Very few entrepreneurs make it big first time round. The secret is to learn from your mistakes, and never give up. Plan for everything you can, but also anticipate failure, and plan ways to deal with it.

Anticipating failure will help you succeed and do things differently and better after learning from the mistakes you made first time round. You succeed by learning from your mistakes.

Innovative and Solution minded

Curiosity and creativity are vital qualities of a successful entrepreneur. Seek to identify opportunities through existing problems, and seek solutions by being creative and innovative. We live in a highly competitive world, and that means you will need to stand out in the crowd. You must therefore think outside the box!

Think outside the box

You must create outstanding products or services, and a strong brand, by being creative and innovative.

But being innovative doesn't necessarily mean that you must create something new. Sometimes you don't need to reinvent the wheel, you can take something that already exists, adapt and refine it, and target it to your customers needs and desires.

Using some of the research and testing the market options outlined in chapter 5 & 6 you can start the journey of making outstanding products or services your customers will love.

Risk taker

Risk-taking is almost synonymous with entrepreneurship. When you embark on your journey of starting and supporting your own business, it will mean putting many things at risk. This may include time spent with your loved ones or even your personal finances.

However, risk should not steer you away from pursuing your dreams and the desire to be your own boss. It is important though, to be aware of the risks involved so that you can prepare and mitigate them. Successful entrepreneurs take calculated risks.

To thrive, understand your terrain, be clued up to all the risks involved, and decide if they are worth taking. Be in charge of your own destiny by planning ahead.

Hard working

The difference between those who make it in business and those that don't is not how hard they work, but how hard and smart they work. Pareto's Principle or the 80/20 rule states that 80% of all results stem from 20% of all sources. In your own business it can mean that if you work smart, 80% of your business can come from 20% of your clients.

Work hard but work smart. You can do this by looking at and analysing all activities you undertake everyday through the lens of the 80/20 rule. Determine which activities are wasting your valuable time, and which are productive. Get rid of activities that are not having any meaningful impact on your business. Don't work hard and be busy just to feel busy and active, carry out meaningful activities.

You can delegate or outsource some of the tasks that you do not have time for, and leverage on other peoples time. For instance there are freelancers with expertise that you may need. Hiring them to do some of the work will free up your valuable time. There are many apps and websites providing freelance services for various tasks from graphic design, video editing, content creation, book keeping etc – the list is endless. In a nutshell, you can find a lot of services on offer online and offline, that can help in the smooth running of your business for a small fee.

To be successful in business you will need to work hard on how to work smarter, be more committed, more focused, and more self disciplined.

Determined to Success

You do not achieve big things by accident. To be successful you must develop better habits, dream big, set big goals, think outside the box, work smart and be determined to succeed. Believe in your dreams and spend less time talking about them, and more time doing them.

I have over time learned what I preach to be true. When I have a project and goals to achieve, I simply put my words into action to achieve my goals in life.

Before I quit my job as a banker in the city of London, I had a desire and vision to empower people with the knowledge I have. At the time something was hindering my vision, I did not have the right skills to train people. That being the case, I was still very determined to one day live my dreams, and nothing was going to get in my way. At one point I put aside everything else and enrolled in college to be a trainer. It was through sheer determination to succeed in what I wanted to do next that saw me through this training program, and I am now doing what I enjoy most, supporting other people through my training and coaching programs *The Movement 4 Lifelong Learning*. Learned knowledge is limited, so visualise and imagine where you want to go, if you can see it in your mind, you can hold it in your hand!

Has a Mentor

Most successful and powerful people have mentors and advisors. Everyone learned their craft from someone, it could be a parent, a teacher, a friend, or a colleague. We all need mentors as good things are rarely accomplished alone.

Having a mentor is hugely important. There is always someone who has successfully done it before you and has more knowledge and experience than you do, and who you can learn from.

Look for a mentor and build a relationship with them, but don't just look for anyone, look for someone who has experience and has walked the walk, someone without a hidden agenda and one who is willing to listen to you and give you their time. If you are lucky to find a good mentor, they can give you the valuable advice and guidance you may need.

Sometimes even an investor can act as a mentor and give you valuable advice, and/or introduce you to the right people for business deals.

Good time management

Time is the currency of modern business. If you manage your time effectively you will improve your productivity.

Stay focused on reducing the amount of time you need to get things done. Learning to have a sense of urgency is the most important quality you can develop with regard to managing your time. When an opportunity presents itself to you, the speed at which you move may determine your success.

To outperform your competitors, you must develop a habit of performing quickly when something must be done. Customers will pay more to get things done fast (think of fast food restaurants). Always meet your customers expectations by meeting agreed deadlines.

Successful people not only work hard but fast. To be successful you need to be disciplined and good at managing your time – getting things done when they should be done. Get rid of unproductive time wasting activities and people in your life if you want to achieve success.

Wisdom

Finally, Have the wisdom to be aware of dreams and passion killers, of energy drainers and time wasters. Those close to you without ambitions, no goals or vision, will be the first to discourage you and bring you down. Have the wisdom and discernment to surround yourself with the right people and always remember that your **Net Worth equals to Networks.**

Use your networks to your advantage, you want them to support your brand. They are your advocates, they are the same people who will talk about your brand and spread the word on your behalf. Having a personable nature will go a long way to help build your brand.

You can do it -Go for it

I hope that reading *Ideas into profit* has inspired you, to take your idea to the next level. Now is the time to recognize your potential, capability and talent that will help you achieve your financial freedom and give you fulfillment.

I wish you all success, wealth and great fulfillment in this journey.

Esther

SUMMARY

- *Develop the entrepreneurial mindset by putting in place some rituals you must perform to succeed, get rid of old rituals that no longer work.*

- *Do what you love doing and are passionate about, think big and plan your business, making the best u se of all the resources you have available, and contin ually seek business opportunities.*

- *Manage your time effectively to maximize success.*

" The way to get started is to quit talking and start doing "

—Walt Disney,
Co-Founder, Disney

Reflections

Power House Global Award 2017 Winner.
Award winning Trainer/Coach/Mentor 2017 London UK.

ABOUT ESTHER

Esther is a UK certified trainer and experiences SME and Financial Literacy coach. She is a winner of two International Awards, for her work that is making impact in communities.

She has a passion to empower women and young people and has been passionately giving back her knowledge in Africa and in United kingdom. Her background is in Banking spanning over several years in the city of London in United Kingdom.

She runs a social enterprise *Movement 4 Lifelong Learning*, part of *Empowering Communities ltd UK*.

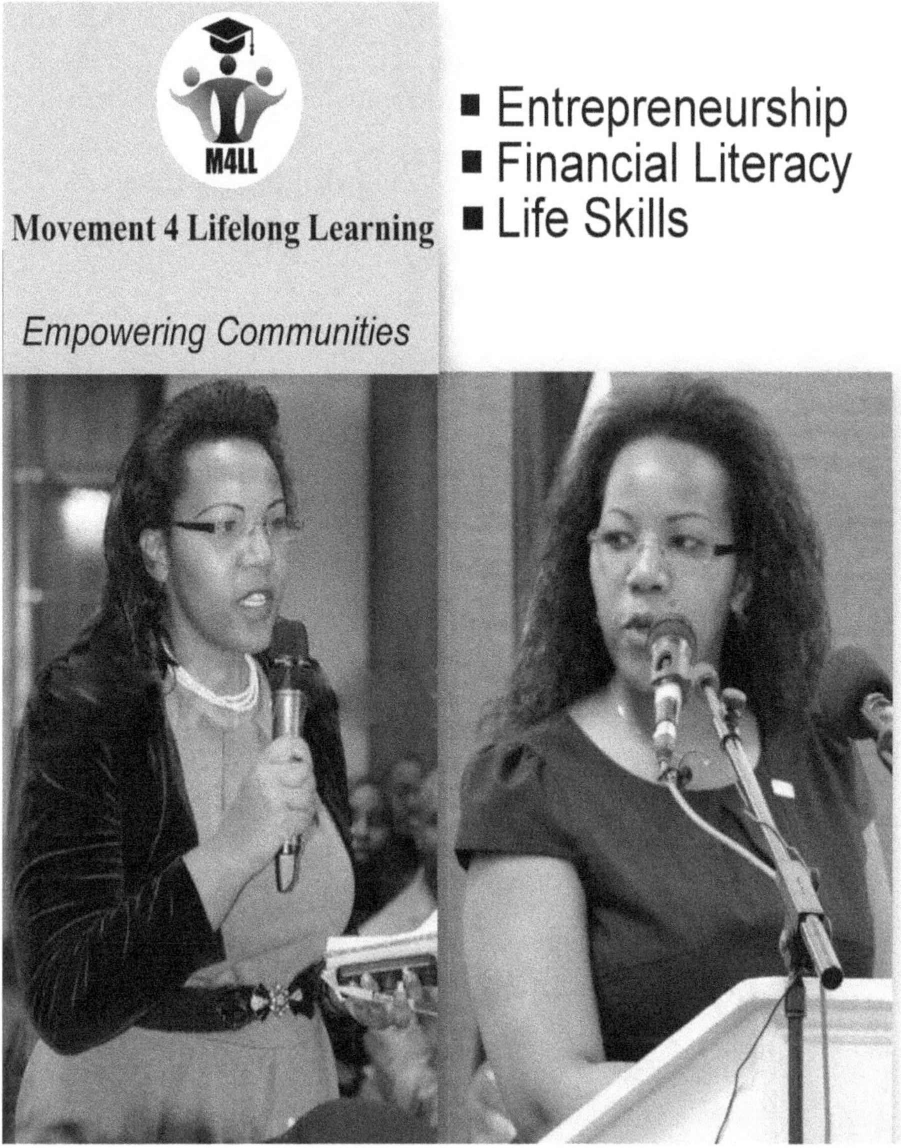

Movement 4 Lifelong Learning

Empowering Communities

- Entrepreneurship
- Financial Literacy
- Life Skills

www.ingramcontent.com/pod-product-compliance
Lightning Source LLC
Chambersburg PA
CBHW071235170526
45165CB00003B/1111